ESSENTIAL ELEMENTS
JAZZ PLAY-ALONG – THE BLUES

By MICHAEL SWEENEY and PAUL MURTHA
Sample Solos by MIKE STEINEL

WELCOME to the exciting world of Jazz Improvisation! Whether you are using this book as a supplement to the **ESSENTIAL ELEMENTS FOR JAZZ ENSEMBLE** m book, or just by itself, this play-along book will help you get started creating your improvised solos. The recordings feature professional jazz players performing v jazz classics and provide an excellent model for playing in a jazz style. In addit **Solos** are provided as a guide for creating effective melodies.

An added feature on the CD-ROM is a software program for changing the tempo of any of the recorded tracks! When used in your computer, **The Amazing Slow Downer** will allow you to adjust the tempo to suit your needs as you progress through the book.

On the CD-ROM, each title appears in two forms:

Split Track/Melody - Complete recording with melody and sample solo. For play-along purposes, <u>Piano Players</u> can eliminate the recorded piano track by turning down the volume on the RIGHT Channel. <u>Bass Players</u> can eliminate the recorded bass track by turning down the volume on the LEFT Channel. The recorded drum track appears on both channels.

Full Stereo/ Rhythm Only - Use this track to play along with the recorded Rhythm Section and create your own solos.

Featured Players:
Jim Farrelly - Alto Sax, Tenor Sax
Jeff Conrad - Trumpet
Loy Hetrick - Trombone
Sandy Williams - Guitar
Steve Allee - Piano
Steve Dokken - Bass
Charleston Sanders - Drums

Recorded at Aire Born Studios, Indianapolis, Indiana

ISBN 978-1-4234-6261-3

HAL•LEONARD®
CORPORATION
7777 W. BLUEMOUND RD. P.O. BOX 13819 MILWAUKEE, WI 53213

ESSENTIAL ELEMENTS
JAZZ PLAY-ALONG – The Blues

EE TEMPO ADJUSTMENT SOFTWARE

Amazing Slow Downer Installation Instructions

The CD-ROM included with this book will function as a normal audio CD. However, to use the tempo adjustment feature, you will need to install **The Amazing Slow Downer** software onto a computer. (Mac users may simply run the program from the disc.)

Note: Amazing Slow Downer requires a multi-session CD-ROM drive to operate. If your computer will only recognize the audio portion of this CD-ROM, you do not have a multi-session capable CD-ROM drive and must upgrade the drive to use this software.

Windows:

- Load the CD-ROM into your CD-ROM Drive.

- Right click and Open or Explore your CD-ROM drive. You should see a folder named "Amazing Slow Downer". If you only see a list of tracks, you are looking at the audio portion of the disk and most likely do not have a multi-session capable CD-ROM drive.

- Open the "Amazing Slow Downer" folder.

- Double-click "Setup_ASD_EE.exe" to install the software from the CD-ROM to your hard disk. Follow the on-screen instructions to complete installation.

- Go to "Start", "Programs" and find the "Amazing Slow Downer EE" folder. Go to that folder and select the "Amazing Slow Downer EE" program.

Macintosh OS 8 and 9:

- Load the CD-ROM into your CD-ROM Drive.

- Double-click on the data portion of the CD-ROM ("EE Software")

- Open the "Amazing OS 8-9" folder.

- Double-click "Amazing Slow Downer EE" to run the software from the CD-ROM, or copy this file to your hard disk and run it from there.

Macintosh OS X:

- Load the CD-ROM into your CD-ROM Drive.

- Double-click on the data portion of the CD-ROM ("EE Software")

- Open the "Amazing OS X" folder.

- Double-click "Amazing X EE" to run the software from the CD-ROM, or copy this file to your hard disk and run it from there.

Note: On Windows NT, 2000 and XP, the user should be logged in as the "Administrator" to guarantee access to the CD-ROM drive. Please see the help file for further information.

THE LANGUAGE OF JAZZ

Jazz music sounds different than traditional or classical music. This is because jazz uses its own unique "language" or style of articulation and phrasing. To help interpret articulation markings in a correct jazz style, the most commonly used markings are listed below. The scat (or vocal) syllables for each type of articulation help to characterize the type of sound to be produced.

Jazz Articulations

These are the four basic articulations in jazz and the related scat syllables for each.

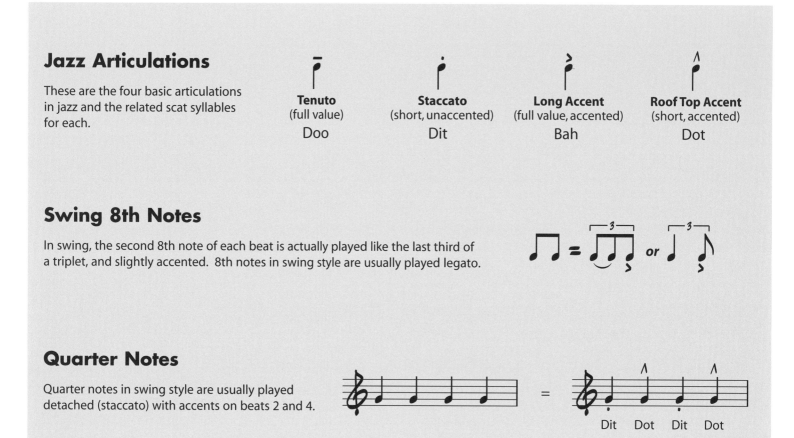

Tenuto (full value)	**Staccato** (short, unaccented)	**Long Accent** (full value, accented)	**Roof Top Accent** (short, accented)
Doo	Dit	Bah	Dot

Swing 8th Notes

In swing, the second 8th note of each beat is actually played like the last third of a triplet, and slightly accented. 8th notes in swing style are usually played legato.

Quarter Notes

Quarter notes in swing style are usually played detached (staccato) with accents on beats 2 and 4.

Dit   Dot   Dit   Dot

STARTING TO IMPROVISE

Improvisation is the process of creating spontaneous melodies based on the harmonies of a particular song. In the beginning, start with the original melody of the song as the basis for creating your own melody. Think of creating variations to this melody by making minor changes to the rhythm or notes. (This was how jazz got started!)

Here are some simple techniques for creating improvisations based on the melody:

1. **Syncopate the melody**. Use the existing notes but change the rhythm.

2. **Adding Rhythms**. Fill in long sustained notes with repeated eighth or quarter notes.

3. **Filling in the Skips**. Skips in the melody can be filled with chromatic or scale notes.

4. **Adding "Wrong" Notes**. A dissonant sounding note (usually a half step off) can sound "jazzy" if it leads into a "good" melody note.

(For a more complete discussion of "Improvising on the Melody" refer to Exercises 51–57 in "Essential Elements for Jazz Ensemble.")

THE BLUES SCALE

There are actually 2 common forms of the *Blues Scale*. These scale types are often used with the *Blues Progression*. Compare these scales with the traditional *Major Scale.*

Major Scale (Concert F)

Blues Scale (Concert F)

Major Blues Scale (Concert F)

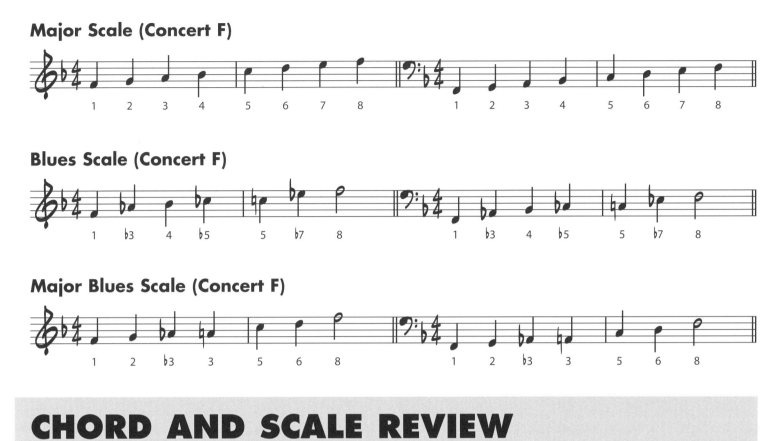

CHORD AND SCALE REVIEW

Listed below are a few common jazz chords and their related scales for improvisation.

Chord Type	Symbol	Related Scale or Mode
Major 7th	FMA7	*F Major Scale*
Dominant 7th	F7	*F Mixolydian (Dominant)*
		F Bebop Scale
Minor 7th	FMI7	*F Dorian Scale*

(For a more complete discussion of how chords and scales are constructed, refer to Exercises 31, 32, 40, 60, 61, 70 and 93 in "Essential Elements for Jazz Ensemble.")

ST. LOUIS BLUES

BY W.C. HANDY

SOLOS (3 CHORUSES)

(SAMPLE VOICINGS)

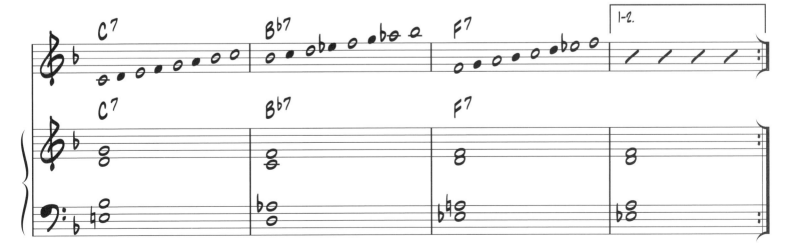

* OPEN NOTEHEADS = CHORD TONES

W.C. HANDY (1873–1958)

Often called "the Father of the Blues", Handy did much to bring the blues to the public as a standard song form. His songs such as *Memphis Blues, St. Louis Blues* and *Beale Street Blues* were commercial successes and became standard parts of early jazz repertoire. Although not the first one to compose the blues, he was the first to write it down for bands to play.

HINTS FOR IMPROVISATION

Repetition is an important element of any jazz solo or composition. The blues often is structured around three repeated phrases with the third being slightly different. The demonstration solo uses this repetitive structure. Try it when improvising your own solos.

GUITAR/PIANO

ST. LOUIS BLUES
SAMPLE SOLO

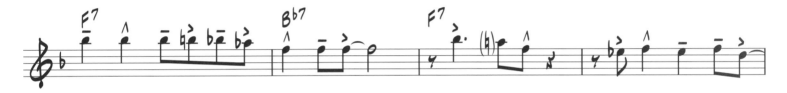

TENOR MADNESS

BY SONNY ROLLINS

CD

③ FULL PERFORMANCE
④ RHYTHM SECTION ONLY

GUITAR/PIANO

* OPEN NOTEHEADS = CHORD TONES

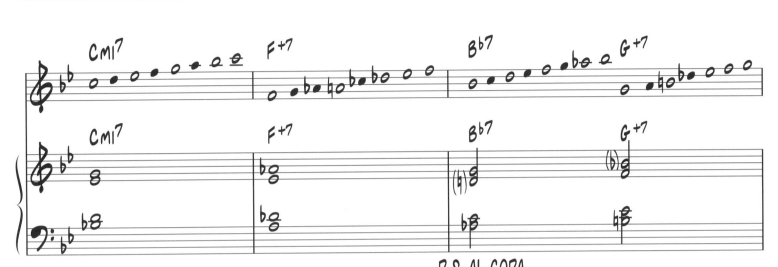

D.S. AL CODA
(TAKE REPEAT)

⊕ CODA

TENOR MADNESS
SAMPLE SOLO

GUITAR/PIANO

SONNY ROLLINS (b.1930)

Rollins is a tenor saxophonist and composer. His long and productive career has included performing and recording with all the great jazz musicians of the last half of the twentieth century. One of his most famous compositions is the calypso styled piece, *St. Thomas*.

HINTS FOR IMPROVISATION

Blues inflection (bending or "smearing" notes) is an important part of soloing. Jazz borrows these blue notes from traditional African music brought to America by slaves. Work to bend and scoop notes to get a characteristic bluesy sound.

BLUE MONK
SAMPLE SOLO

GUITAR/PIANO

THELONIOUS MONK (1917–1982)

Pianist and composer Thelonious Monk was one of the true giants of modern jazz. He developed an extremely personal piano style and contributed to the jazz repertoire some of the most popular and often recorded compositions. He is one of five musicians to be featured on the cover of *Time* magazine.

HINTS FOR IMPROVISATION

Jazz phrasing is an important part of any jazz solo or composition. Notice in the sample solo that most of the phrases start and stop on the upbeat, not the downbeat. This is very common in jazz. Try it in your own solos and you will sound "jazzy."t

CD
☐ ❺ FULL PERFORMANCE
☐ ❻ RHYTHM SECTION ONLY
GUITAR/PIANO

BLUE MONK

B♭ MAJOR BLUES SCALE

BY THELONIOUS MONK

* OPEN NOTEHEADS = CHORD TONES

BLUES IN HOSS FLAT

CD

7 FULL PERFORMANCE

8 RHYTHM SECTION ONLY

GUITAR/PIANO

WORDS AND MUSIC BY
WILLIAM "COUNT" BASIE
AND FRANK FOSTER

SOLOS (3 CHORUSES)

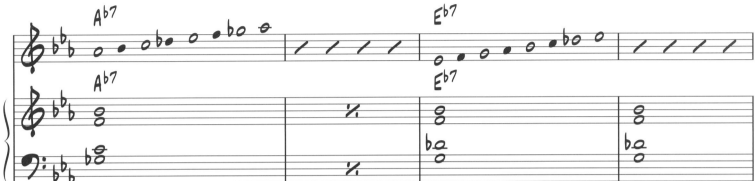

D.S. AL CODA
(TAKE REPEAT)

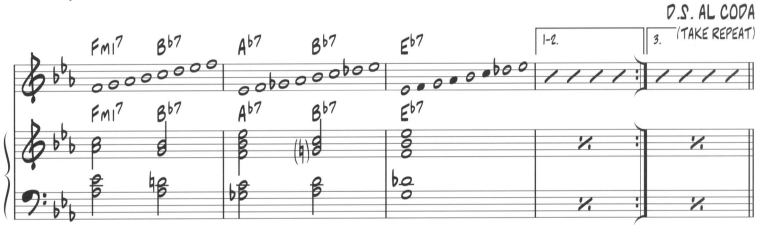

* OPEN NOTEHEADS = CHORD TONES

GUITAR/PIANO

BLUES IN HOSS FLAT
SAMPLE SOLO

FRANK FOSTER (1928–2011)

Frank Foster was a saxophonist and composer who had a long association with the Count Basie Orchestra. He contributed both arrangements and original compositions to the Basie band and after Basie's death, lead the band from 1986 to 1995.

HINTS FOR IMPROVISATION

A good solo is like a good story; it should build and maintain interest. One way this is done in music is through the use of "register". Notice how the sample solo builds gradually into the upper register (over the course of three choruses). Try that when soloing. Wait to use your high notes until later in the solo.

COLD DUCK TIME

Bb BLUES SCALE

BY EDDIE HARRIS

CD
◆ 9 FULL PERFORMANCE
◆ 10 RHYTHM SECTION ONLY

GUITAR/PIANO

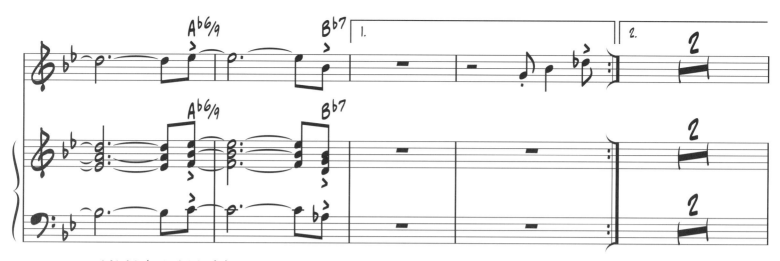

SOLOS (3 CHORUSES)

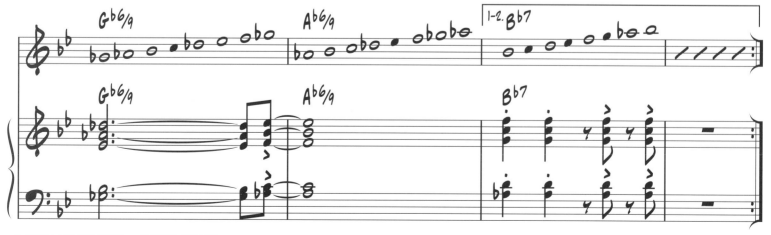

* OPEN NOTEHEADS = CHORD TONES

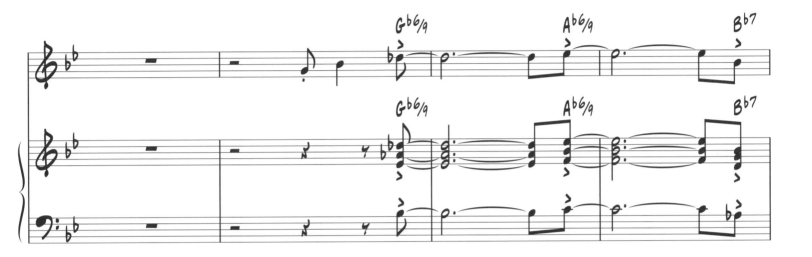

EDDIE HARRIS (1934–1996)

Harris was a highly innovative composer and saxophonist who helped fuse rock elements with jazz in the 1960s. His composition, *Cold Duck Time*, appeared on one of the classic jazz albums of all time, *Swiss Movement*, a live recording made with Les McCann at the Montreaux Jazz Festival in 1969.

HINTS FOR IMPROVISATION

This song is played in a "straight 8th" style, so often the 8th-notes will be detached and more of equal value than in swing music. Pay particular attention to the suggested articulations in the sample solo.

COLD DUCK TIME
SAMPLE SOLO

GUITAR/PIANO

GUITAR/PIANO

STRAIGHT NO CHASER
SAMPLE SOLO

THELONIOUS MONK (1917–1982)

Monk is often regarded as one of the founders of bebop, but his style is somewhat different from typical bebop. His compositions and playing are full of dissonant harmonies, extended use of space, angularity and blues-influenced riffs.

HINTS FOR IMPROVISATION

Rhythmic displacement is the technique of repeating a rhythm but in a different part of the bar. The melody of *Straight No Chaser* and the first chorus of the demonstration solo does this. This creates rhythmic interest. Try it in your own solos and compositions.

STRAIGHT NO CHASER

CD

🎵 FULL PERFORMANCE
🎵 RHYTHM SECTION ONLY

GUITAR/PIANO

BY THELONIOUS MONK

SOLOS (3 CHORUSES)

(SAMPLE VOICINGS)

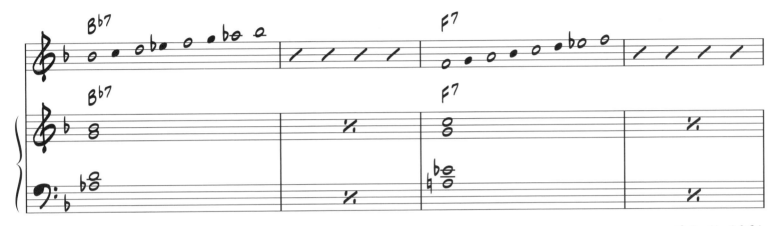

D.S. AL CODA
(TAKE REPEAT)

CODA

* OPEN NOTEHEADS = CHORD TONES

ALL BLUES

BY MILES DAVIS

GUITAR/PIANO

ALL BLUES
SAMPLE SOLO

MILES DAVIS (1926–1991)

Miles was one of the most influential musicians of the twentieth century. He was a driving force in the development of bebop, cool jazz, hard bop, modal jazz and fusion. He also had a great gift at discovering talented young players and mentoring them.

HINTS FOR IMPROVISATION

All Blues is written in 3/4 time which can be very challenging when you first try to improvise in it. Try to keep the melody of the song going in your head while you solo so you can keep your place. Once you feel the important downbeats where the chords change and are able to adjust the melodies to fit, you can free up a bit.

GUITAR/PIANO

BLUES IN THE CLOSET
SAMPLE SOLO

OSCAR PETTIFORD (1922–1960)

Pettiford was an important bassist with many great swing era and bebop players such as Coleman Hawkins, Ben Webster, Dizzy Gillespie and Duke Ellington. He also pioneered the use of cello as a jazz instrument.

HINTS FOR IMPROVISATION

The melody of *Blues in the Closet* demonstrates one of the most common techniques of blues composition and soloing: the "roving 3rd." Notice how the melody is repetitious but uses both the raised and lowered 3rd of the key. This is done to make the melody fit with the chord progression. Try it in your own soloing.

Blues in the Closet

CD

15 FULL PERFORMANCE
16 RHYTHM SECTION ONLY

G BLUES SCALE   G MAJOR BLUES SCALE

GUITAR/PIANO

BY OSCAR PETTIFORD

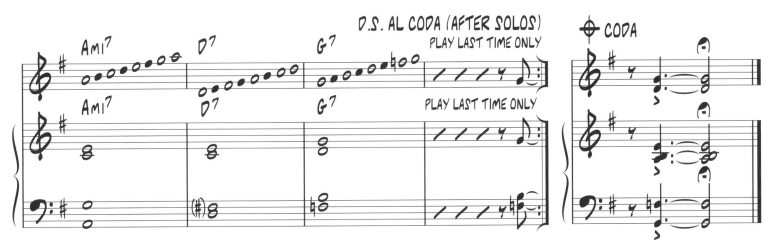

* OPEN NOTEHEADS = CHORD TONES

BAGS' GROOVE

CD

17 FULL PERFORMANCE
18 RHYTHM SECTION ONLY

GUITAR/PIANO

F BLUES SCALE

BY MILT JACKSON

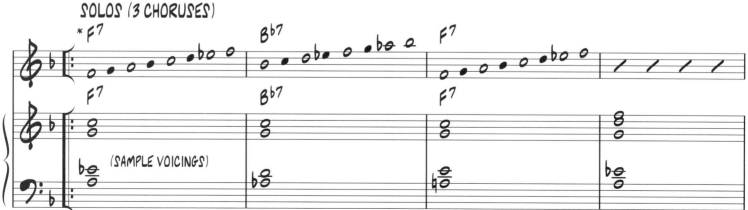

SOLOS (3 CHORUSES)

(SAMPLE VOICINGS)

* OPEN NOTEHEADS = CHORD TONES

D.S. AL CODA
(TAKE REPEAT)

GUITAR/PIANO

BAGS' GROOVE
SAMPLE SOLO

MILT JACKSON (1923–1999)

Milt Jackson was a vibes player who worked and recorded with the most important figures of the modern jazz era including Miles Davis, Dizzy Gillespie, Thelonious Monk and Charlie Parker. He was also one of the founders of the Modern Jazz Quartet, a very successful group that also included John Lewis and Percy Heath.

HINTS FOR IMPROVISATION

Bags' Groove is a great example of a blues using a simple 4-bar repeated melody. There are hundreds of melodies like this in jazz. Search them out, learn them and use them in your blues solos. These are sometimes called "riffs" and they are an important part of any jazz solo .

GUITAR/PIANO

BLUE 'N' BOOGIE
SAMPLE SOLO

DIZZY GILLESPIE (1917–1993)

Along with Charlie Parker, trumpeter Dizzy Gillespie was one of the main innovators of bebop, a style of music developed in the 1940s. Although Dizzy became very recognizable for his puffed-out cheeks, his bent horn, and onstage antics, he was a serious musician whose contributions as a player and composer are truly significant.

HINTS FOR IMPROVISATION

Good swing feel is important when playing solos as well as when playing section figures. Remember to accent "2 and 4" when playing quarter and 8th-notes that are not on the beat (on the "and"). Remember some quarters can be played detached with a slight "tongue stop" at the end of the note.

BLUE 'N' BOOGIE

GUITAR/PIANO

BY JOHN "DIZZY" GILLESPIE
AND FRANK PAPARELLI

SOLOS (3 CHORUSES)

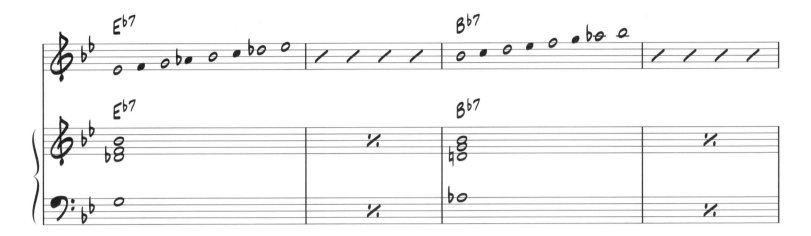

(SAMPLE VOICINGS)

D.C. AL CODA
(TAKE REPEAT)

CODA

* OPEN NOTEHEADS = CHORD TONES

ST. LOUIS BLUES

CD

⏵ FULL PERFORMANCE

⏵ RHYTHM SECTION ONLY

BY W.C. HANDY

BASS

W.C. HANDY (1873–1958)

Often called "the Father of the Blues", Handy did much to bring the blues to the public as a standard song form. His songs such as *Memphis Blues*, *St. Louis Blues* and *Beale Street Blues* were commercial successes and became standard parts of early jazz repertoire. Although not the first one to compose the blues, he was the first to write it down for bands to play.

HINTS FOR IMPROVISATION

Repetition is an important element of any jazz solo or composition. The blues often is structured around three repeated phrases with the third being slightly different. The demonstration solo uses this repetitive structure. Try it when improvising your own solos.

TENOR MADNESS

BY SONNY ROLLINS

CD

❸ FULL PERFORMANCE
❹ RHYTHM SECTION ONLY

BASS

SONNY ROLLINS (b.1930)

Rollins is a tenor saxophonist and composer. His long tend productive career has included performing and recording with all the great jazz musicians of the last half of the twentieth century. One of his most famous compositions is the calypso styled piece, *St. Thomas.*

HINTS FOR IMPROVISATION

Blues inflection (bending or "smearing" notes) is an important part of soloing. Jazz borrows these blue notes from traditional African music brought to America by slaves. Work to bend and scoop notes to get a characteristic bluesy sound.

42

BLUE MONK

BY THELONIOUS MONK

THELONIOUS MONK (1917–1982)

Pianist and composer Thelonious Monk was one of the true giants of modern jazz. He developed an extremely personal piano style and contributed to the jazz repertoire some of the most popular and often recorded compositions. He is one of five musicians to be featured on the cover of *Time* magazine.

HINTS FOR IMPROVISATION

Jazz phrasing is an important part of any jazz solo or composition. Notice in the sample solo that most of the phrases start and stop on the upbeat, not the downbeat. This is very common in jazz. Try it in your own solos and you will sound "jazzy."t

BLUES IN HOSS FLAT

CD

▶ FULL PERFORMANCE

◆ 8 RHYTHM SECTION ONLY

WORDS AND MUSIC BY
WILLIAM "COUNT" BASIE
AND FRANK FOSTER

BASS

FRANK FOSTER (1928–2011)

Frank Foster was a saxophonist and composer who had a long association with the Count Basie Orchestra. He contributed both arrangements and original compositions to the Basie band and after Basie's death, lead the band from 1986 to 1995.

HINTS FOR IMPROVISATION

A good solo is like a good story; it should build and maintain interest. One way this is done in music is through the use of "register". Notice how the sample solo builds gradually into the upper register (over the course of three choruses). Try that when soloing. Wait to use your high notes until later in the solo.

COLD DUCK TIME

BY EDDIE HARRIS

EDDIE HARRIS (1934–1996)

Harris was a highly innovative composer and saxophonist who helped fuse rock elements with jazz in the 1960s. His composition, *Cold Duck Time*, appeared on one of the classic jazz albums of all time, *Swiss Movement*, a live recording made with Les McCann at the Montreaux Jazz Festival in 1969.

HINTS FOR IMPROVISATION

This song is played in a "straight 8th" style, so often the 8th-notes will be detached and more of equal value than in swing music. Pay particular attention to the suggested articulations in the sample solo.

STRAIGHT NO CHASER

CD
- ⑪ FULL PERFORMANCE
- ⑫ RHYTHM SECTION ONLY

BASS

BY THELONIOUS MONK

SOLOS (3 CHORUSES)

(SAMPLE BASS LINE)

THELONIOUS MONK (1917–1982)

Monk is often regarded as one of the founders of bebop, but his style is somewhat different from typical bebop. His compositions and playing are full of dissonant harmonies, extended use of space, angularity and blues-influenced riffs.

HINTS FOR IMPROVISATION

Rhythmic displacement is the technique of repeating a rhythm but in a different part of the bar. The melody of *Straight No Chaser* and the first chorus of the demonstration solo does this. This creates rhythmic interest. Try it in your own solos and compositions.

ALL BLUES

CD
13 FULL PERFORMANCE
14 RHYTHM SECTION ONLY

BASS

BY MILES DAVIS

MILES DAVIS (1926–1991)

Miles was one of the most influential musicians of the twentieth century. He was a driving force in the development of bebop, cool jazz, hard bop, modal jazz and fusion. He also had a great gift at discovering talented young players and mentoring them.

HINTS FOR IMPROVISATION

All Blues is written in 3/4 time which can be very challenging when you first try to improvise in it. Try to keep the melody of the song going in your head while you solo so you can keep your place. Once you feel the important downbeats where the chords change and are able to adjust the melodies to fit, you can free up a bit.

BLUES IN THE CLOSET

CD

15 FULL PERFORMANCE
16 RHYTHM SECTION ONLY

BASS

BY OSCAR PETTIFORD

SOLOS (3 CHORUSES)

(SAMPLE BASS LINE)

TO CODA

D.S. AL CODA (AFTER SOLOS)

CODA

OSCAR PETTIFORD (1922–1960)

Pettiford was an important bassist with many great swing era and bebop players such as Coleman Hawkins, Ben Webster, Dizzy Gillespie and Duke Ellington. He also pioneered the use of cello as a jazz instrument.

HINTS FOR IMPROVISATION

The melody of *Blues in the Closet* demonstrates one of the most common techniques of blues composition and soloing: the "roving 3rd." Notice how the melody is repetitious but uses both the raised and lowered 3rd of the key. This is done to make the melody fit with the chord progression. Try it in your own soloing.

BAGS' GROOVE

CD

17 FULL PERFORMANCE
18 RHYTHM SECTION ONLY

BASS

BY MILT JACKSON

MILT JACKSON (1923–1999)

Milt Jackson was a vibes player who worked and recorded with the most important figures of the modern jazz era including Miles Davis, Dizzy Gillespie, Thelonious Monk and Charlie Parker. He was also one of the founders of the Modern Jazz Quartet, a very successful group that also included John Lewis and Percy Heath.

HINTS FOR IMPROVISATION

Bags' Groove is a great example of a blues using a simple 4-bar repeated melody. There are hundreds of melodies like this in jazz. Search them out, learn them and use them in your blues solos. These are sometimes called "riffs" and they are an important part of any jazz solo .

BLUE 'N' BOOGIE

BY JOHN "DIZZY" GILLESPIE
AND FRANK PAPARELLI

CD

FULL PERFORMANCE

RHYTHM SECTION ONLY

BASS

DIZZY GILLESPIE (1917–1993)

Along with Charlie Parker, trumpeter Dizzy Gillespie was one of the main innovators of bebop, a style of music developed in the 1940s. Although Dizzy became very recognizable for his puffed-out cheeks, his bent horn, and onstage antics, he was a serious musician whose contributions as a player and composer are truly significant.

HINTS FOR IMPROVISATION

Good swing feel is important when playing solos as well as when playing section figures. Remember to accent "2 and 4" when playing quarter and 8th-notes that are not on the beat (on the "and"). Remember some quarters can be played detached with a slight "tongue stop" at the end of the note.

St. Louis Blues

BY W.C. HANDY

DRUMS

W.C. HANDY (1873–1958)

Often called "the Father of the Blues", Handy did much to bring the blues to the public as a standard song form. His songs such as *Memphis Blues, St. Louis Blues* and *Beale Street Blues* were commercial successes and became standard parts of early jazz repertoire. Although not the first one to compose the blues, he was the first to write it down for bands to play.

HINTS FOR IMPROVISATION

Repetition is an important element of any jazz solo or composition. The blues often is structured around three repeated phrases with the third being slightly different. The demonstration solo uses this repetitive structure. Try it when improvising your own solos.

TENOR MADNESS

CD
③ FULL PERFORMANCE
④ RHYTHM SECTION ONLY

BY SONNY ROLLINS

DRUMS

SONNY ROLLINS (b.1930)

Rollins is a tenor saxophonist and composer. His long and productive career has included performing and recording with all the great jazz musicians of the last half of the twentieth century. One of his most famous compositions is the calypso styled piece, *St. Thomas*.

HINTS FOR IMPROVISATION

Blues inflection (bending or "smearing" notes) is an important part of soloing. Jazz borrows these blue notes from traditional African music brought to America by slaves. Work to bend and scoop notes to get a characteristic bluesy sound.

BLUE MONK

CD

◆5 FULL PERFORMANCE
◆6 RHYTHM SECTION ONLY

BY THELONIOUS MONK

DRUMS

THELONIOUS MONK (1917–1982)

Pianist and composer Thelonious Monk was one of the true giants of modern jazz. He developed an extremely personal piano style and contributed to the jazz repertoire some of the most popular and often recorded compositions. He is one of five musicians to be featured on the cover of *Time* magazine.

HINTS FOR IMPROVISATION

Jazz phrasing is an important part of any jazz solo or composition. Notice in the sample solo that most of the phrases start and stop on the upbeat, not the downbeat. This is very common in jazz. Try it in your own solos and you will sound "jazzy."

BLUES IN HOSS FLAT

WORDS AND MUSIC BY
WILLIAM "COUNT" BASIE
AND FRANK FOSTER

FRANK FOSTER (1928–2011)

Frank Foster was a saxophonist and composer who had a long association with the Count Basie Orchestra. He contributed both arrangements and original compositions to the Basie band and after Basie's death, lead the band from 1986 to 1995.

HINTS FOR IMPROVISATION

A good solo is like a good story; it should build and maintain interest. One way this is done in music is through the use of "register". Notice how the sample solo builds gradually into the upper register (over the course of three choruses). Try that when soloing. Wait to use your high notes until later in the solo.

CD

COLD DUCK TIME

BY EDDIE HARRIS

DRUMS

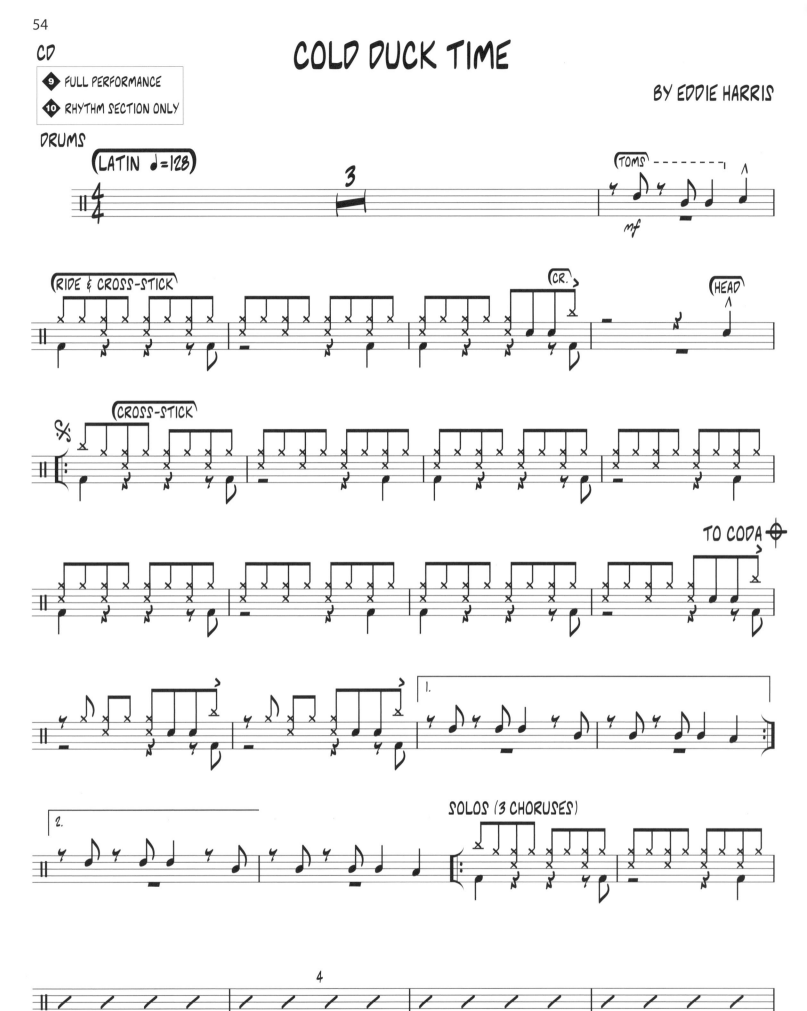

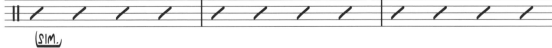

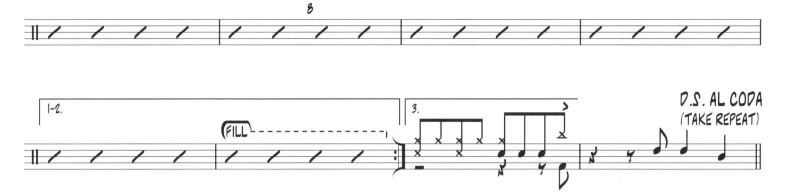

EDDIE HARRIS (1934–1996)

Harris was a highly innovative composer and saxophonist who helped fuse rock elements with jazz in the 1960s. His composition, *Cold Duck Time*, appeared on one of the classic jazz albums of all time, *Swiss Movement*, a live recording made with Les McCann at the Montreaux Jazz Festival in 1969.

HINTS FOR IMPROVISATION

This song is played in a "straight 8th" style, so often the 8th-notes will be detached and more of equal value than in swing music. Pay particular attention to the suggested articulations in the sample solo.

CD

11 FULL PERFORMANCE

12 RHYTHM SECTION ONLY

STRAIGHT NO CHASER

DRUMS

BY THELONIOUS MONK

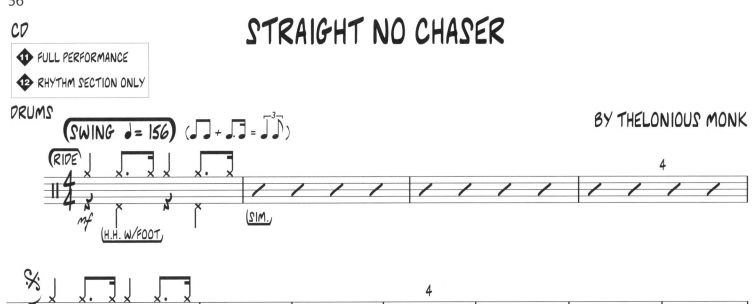

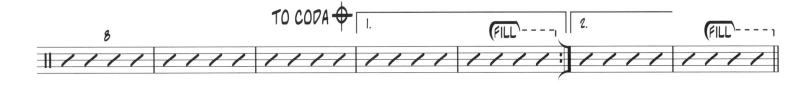

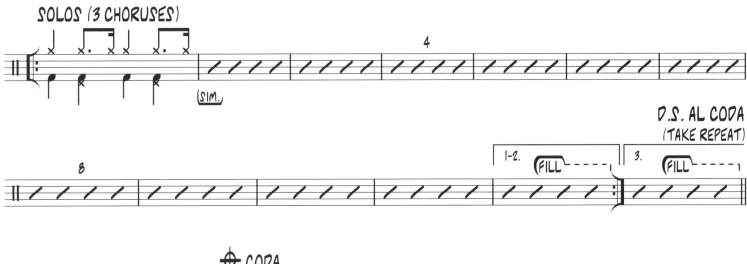

THELONIOUS MONK (1917–1982)

Monk is often regarded as one of the founders of bebop, but his style is somewhat different from typical bebop. His compositions and playing are full of dissonant harmonies, extended use of space, angularity and blues-influenced riffs.

HINTS FOR IMPROVISATION

Rhythmic displacement is the technique of repeating a rhythm but in a different part of the bar. The melody of *Straight No Chaser* and the first chorus of the demonstration solo does this. This creates rhythmic interest. Try it in your own solos and compositions.

ALL BLUES

CD

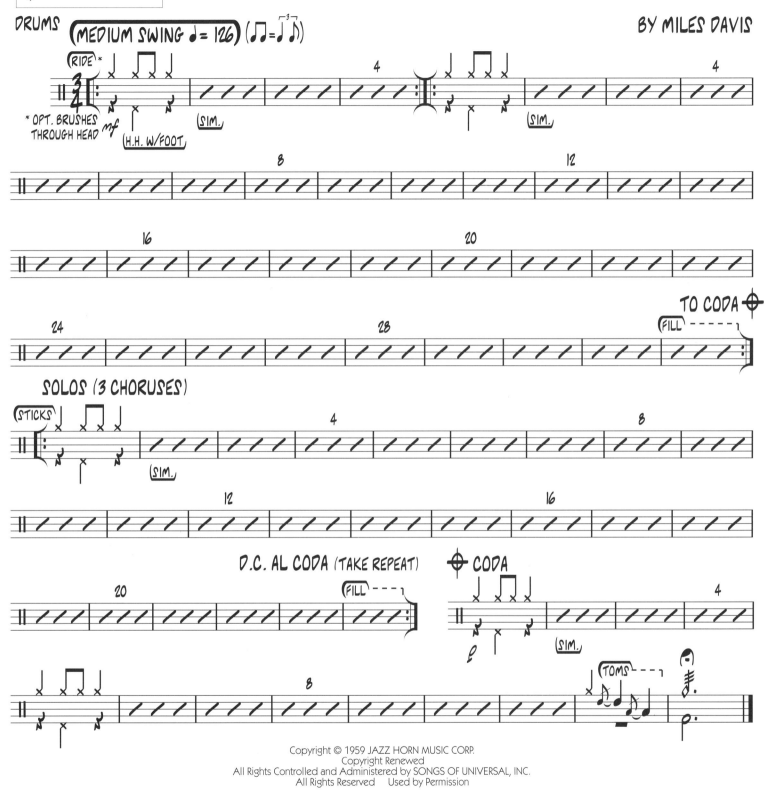

By Miles Davis

MILES DAVIS (1926–1991)

Miles was one of the most influential musicians of the twentieth century. He was a driving force in the development of bebop, cool jazz, hard bop, modal jazz and fusion. He also had a great gift at discovering talented young players and mentoring them.

HINTS FOR IMPROVISATION

All Blues is written in 3/4 time which can be very challenging when you first try to improvise in it. Try to keep the melody of the song going in your head while you solo so you can keep your place. Once you feel the important downbeats where the chords change and are able to adjust the melodies to fit, you can free up a bit.

BLUES IN THE CLOSET

CD

15 FULL PERFORMANCE
16 RHYTHM SECTION ONLY

DRUMS

BY OSCAR PETTIFORD

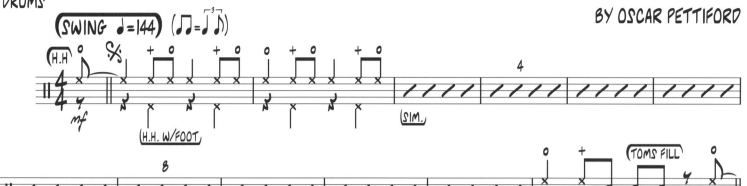

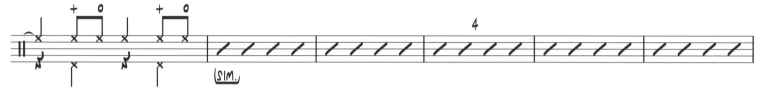

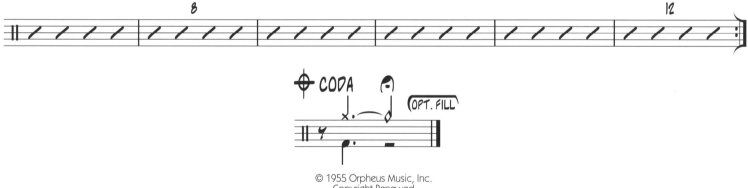

OSCAR PETTIFORD (1922–1960)

Pettiford was an important bassist with many great swing era and bebop players such as Coleman Hawkins, Ben Webster, Dizzy Gillespie and Duke Ellington. He also pioneered the use of cello as a jazz instrument.

HINTS FOR IMPROVISATION

The melody of *Blues in the Closet* demonstrates one of the most common techniques of blues composition and soloing: the "roving 3rd." Notice how the melody is repetitious but uses both the raised and lowered 3rd of the key. This is done to make the melody fit with the chord progression. Try it in your own soloing.

BAGS' GROOVE

CD

DRUMS

BY MILT JACKSON

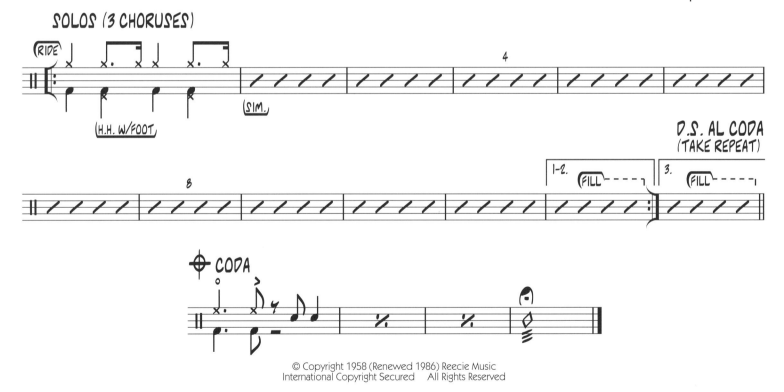

MILT JACKSON (1923–1999)

Milt Jackson was a vibes player who worked and recorded with the most important figures of the modern jazz era including Miles Davis, Dizzy Gillespie, Thelonious Monk and Charlie Parker. He was also one of the founders of the Modern Jazz Quartet, a very successful group that also included John Lewis and Percy Heath.

HINTS FOR IMPROVISATION

Bags' Groove is a great example of a blues using a simple 4-bar repeated melody. There are hundreds of melodies like this in jazz. Search them out, learn them and use them in your blues solos. These are sometimes called "riffs" and they are an important part of any jazz solo .

BLUE 'N' BOOGIE

BY JOHN "DIZZY" GILLESPIE
AND FRANK PAPARELLI

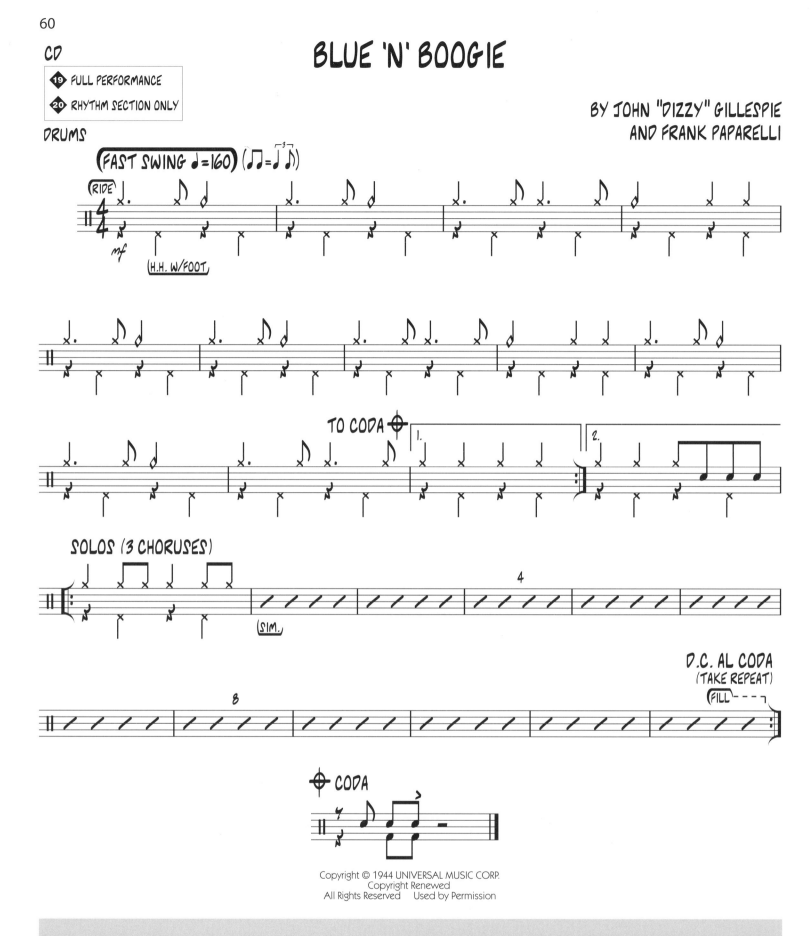

DIZZY GILLESPIE (1917–1993)

Along with Charlie Parker, trumpeter Dizzy Gillespie was one of the main innovators of bebop, a style of music developed in the 1940s. Although Dizzy became very recognizable for his puffed-out cheeks, his bent horn, and onstage antics, he was a serious musician whose contributions as a player and composer are truly significant.

HINTS FOR IMPROVISATION

Good swing feel is important when playing solos as well as when playing section figures. Remember to accent "2 and 4" when playing quarter and 8th-notes that are not on the beat (on the "and"). Remember some quarters can be played detached with a slight "tongue stop" at the end of the note.